CO

KUHL HOUSE POETS

edited by Mark Levine and Ben Doyle

complex sleep

POEMS BY TONY TOST

UNIVERSITY OF IOWA PRESS   IOWA CITY

University of Iowa Press, Iowa City 52242
www.uiowapress.org
Printed in the United States of America

Design by Richard Hendel

The University of Iowa Press is a member of Green Press
Initiative and is committed to preserving natural resources.

Printed on acid-free paper

Library of Congress Cataloging-in-Publication Data
Tost, Tony.
Complex sleep: poems / by Tony Tost.
    p.   cm.—(Kuhl house poets)
ISBN-13: 978-1-58729-621-5
ISBN-10: 1-58729-621-7
I. Title.
PS3620.O88C66 2007
811'.6—dc22   2007007355

07 08 09 10 11 P 5 4 3 2 1

for Leigh

CONTENTS

ACKNOWLEDGMENTS

A number of these writings were previously published or excerpted
in the following journals: "Imaginary Synonyms": *Hambone;*
"Squint": *Damn the Caesars;* "A Northern Eros": *Verse;* "Ink Drop":
Word for/Word; "An Emperor's Nostalgia: a Dozen for Leigh":
Mandorla, O Poss; "Complex Sleep": *Backwards City, Filling Station,
H_NGM_N, The Hat,* and *Talisman;* and "Timeless": *Drunken Boat.*
World Jelly was published as a chapbook by Effing Press. Praise to
Scott Pierce.
"Complex Sleep" was published as a chapbook in *Black Warrior Review*
Vol. 32, #2,
This book was written in the companionship of Nic Pizzolatto,
Tim Van Dyke, and the Lucifer Poetics Group. Additional
thanks to Ben Doyle for his patience, friendship, and judgment.

Further, why do we say that the word "tree"—spoken or written—is a symbol to us for trees? Both the word itself and trees themselves enter into our experience on equal terms; and it would be just as sensible, viewing the question abstractedly, for trees to symbolize the word "tree" as for the word to symbolize the trees.

This is certainly true, and human nature sometimes works that way. For example, if you are a poet and wish to write a lyric on trees, you will walk into the forest in order that the trees may suggest the appropriate words. Thus for the poet in his ecstasy—or perhaps, agony—of composition the trees are the symbols and the words are the meaning. He concentrates on the trees in order to get at the words.

But most of us are not poets, though we read their lyrics with proper respect.

—Alfred North Whitehead

COMPLEX SLEEP

IMAGINARY SYNONYMS

Eventually we take it apart

dissecting it palate by plate

only to get smaller

your mother asks me to tell her

what to think of when she says "milk"

and you say Waves

of punishment, of possibility

a rush now always on

secondary phenomena. Come home

bring goldfish for the

ponds. Cleft angels

distorted talons

stuck with the shapes we are

as waves. A cave. A nimbus

around my brother as he hums

home. Seduction of the sources

the first days of being enormous

analogous holograph of

above. My medium is

filled by quanta wants

heating the nonluminous iron bar

inner sight. Granular

the syllables are syllabic

if mouthed. Come home

to discrete levels of comfort

grief may be rotting half my brain

but I remember all of your face

faintly. An observer

you enter these memories

grief understands the poses

it is to assume. The film passes

through the gate

undulates in ways sound does

away from pronouncement. This

the very womb of evasion

the crest of each wave emits

a portrait unleashed

static enfolded in known formation

aeon overcome by error

shoulders heaving, mouth open

and moving. Come home

your father's birthday is today

for Kim Sun-il

Far from being, the music is already there, near the beginning, nearer everything.

Then a choir, what of the mind, the owl and the eagle, can you tremble.

The meadow moved, in the wind, and in the dead of night, the boys broke.

Your lips trembled, there is no unknown, stranger remember, the sky is spangled.

Here in the snow, we heard Scripture, her dress was a thousand years, only the door to a room.

There are no insides, so the hen laid the egg, it doesn't want to eat, and I don't want a word.

To think about them almost, so they greet me, who believes the operation, the first day lilies.

It is a book of half, only the insane wish, by now the orphans sounding, Isaiah gnawed his tongue.

That is the book, the basic act is exterior, this is measured, by the first things.

The undisputed meter, the optic nerve system, the psychic stretch of sight, or rather its imbalance.

Our talk gets its meaning, haven't they gone wrong, does a child believe, doubt itself rests.

The great fright has turned, the person sitting opposite, and the miracle is, as long as this is.

One would like to return, that principle of order, we neither console nor promise, in the crossing.

The local strays have evolved, they are outside time, we feel a kinship, the radial lines.

We are in the throes, this is our primal scene, in ascent the mystic is, then the image was.

The book of nature, sitting in a closet, now before it appears, the circumference assembles.

It made itself, or perhaps it has always been, that is the usual extent, it is not a dilemma.

They came as apparitions, the truck cast its own, my mother outlined, in unquiet she sits.

All these facts fit, to live we do need facts, for they do not interfere, as they are in flux.

A blanket was strung, her hands fresh from the burial, she was in the boat, with a half mile of sea.

In view of the marked, observing the Spanish, meantime the whole host, it was the echo.

There's no mention of deception, what is my difference, under the street lamps, still on the stairs.

He went to the window, almost involuntarily, it was drizzling, here if anywhere.

To write the disappearing, these second realities, the last night gnashing, in the unfolding.

A prick from a rose, the place of decision, I am not speaking, trying to resist.

What is a stutter, those tracks are signs, the imagination beholds, the god of fragments.

For it is the closeness, listening to the endless, the energy wants us, it breaks beyond.

She carried thought, a practiced austerity, the human face in repose, begins the disappearing.

The problem with syntax, the problem with giving, she stood on one foot, and imagined a future.

There are maps of the earth, and we are in the real, it has all gone emptied, it doesn't seem urgent.

Like a hunter who walks, under the luminous, as it is a huge banner, you pass your hand under.

The passage asks, the fusion of dream, our clarity follows, the meadow is named.

Late at night the ringing, if only one could be giving, begins in the shifting, this heap of hope.

The goal is far distant, it becomes the wind, one is often its child, of its inner eye.

She creates an echo, I lack a reflection, those eerie lines, this black dot.

So the book remains, pages come calling, they must have lain in water, the eternal words.

They come to the water, the summer is greening, I saw a girl with a lamp, her mystery trained.

Everything as processed, leaving its look within us, as we were the desert, as we had no borders.

Here are the fires, to permit the book, to be perfected, by the wind.

The dark is housed, and another ballad, the human voice emerging, the impossible tape.

Who cupped my ear, tattered wisps of clouds, didn't Papa go up, through the inner gate.

Could Nature be headless, revival of the snake, the specific bridge, the river sometimes gathers.

A photograph of Socrates, and his tongue removed, who swam out and signaled, it is both person and tree.

The rain we thought, a solution not ready, annoyed you bit, who covered his mouth.

We have caught everything, the boat is called, at night a train, or
  perhaps bouquets.

The whitened tops, exploding horizontal, the sun is scratched, the
  flow of the line.

Plain song madrigal, love moves in bodies, voiced from the throat,
  the ascending smoke.

And the antiphonal, a father rejoicing, he goes on kindling, with no
  one around.

And now at glances, the complex blossoms, but Moth's eyes see, they
  only ring.

The farce hurts, the errors multiply, still the divining, remember the
  keepers.

But who has a parent, dark pools of blood, if a truth is uttered, there
  are no hours.

Winter he says, the hour at hand, how large a body, the exacting cost.

The keepers of vision, their miracle beasts, also the ravens, the
  demons drive.

There is the breathtaking, our tables shimmer, what of the enduring,
  and the whipping post.

It is one of the last acts, dark oak branches, the tree comes down, and
  thereby hangs.

What bright poppies, so many more shades, and treading the steps,
  the threshing floor.

For I dreamt not this, not at all to hammer, the usual boundary,
  fitting together.

And thought is moved, for what is marked, and killing an animal,
  which brings us home.

Tantalized ghosts, touched with paint, in each other like combs, of
  what never fades.

The roof and its corners, the noumenal places, rain in its season, searches for its twin.

Along the avenue, inured to heights, sleeves in my hand, cicada in my vest.

The chain of rebirth, an infant series, mute significance, assumes another form.

A canopy of skin, another jokes of it, language in the sky, is the sun again.

In our own sector, fires of the Spirits, their particular colors, black honey from Brazil.

Time need not enter, as a manifest idea, the accuracy of an eye, we accept as fixed.

What emerges from trees, and more red teeth, a given orange light, thought by others.

Artificial lighting, among tree shadows, folds of flesh, in houses shift.

Her paper face, and other beginnings, all the black letters, heroic and alone.

Victory there, and you can't get out, frame to frame, from the stone.

But behind the words, who feels its knifing, an infant's siring, a dog at my heels.

In the fine mist, rain is falling, it was black or white, crying out of my veins.

The mercy of winds, the navel of an ape, the end of the flesh, it was the mercy.

The animal about the blossoms
sang for them in the drifting
who also matter to us

You will receive yours
beneath the blanket

It is rising rude tinting
too late to cut the year in half
sparing nothing

Come here and help me
little levee
with your lamb

There is a wandering before me
now my burdens
I believe the crazy face

Waiting

Nothing morning

Resist the successful statement
almost intelligently
a nail in the wall
there hang the bearings

So that is what I do

Riders finding joy in the sunlight
on the face of the earth

Attention is
the animal behind
the immediate

Asshole serpent
write this down

Reckless skater
is there nothing for your gases
to push against

Speech hates you too
I don't know
how to love the whole

Words are magic
because they hang
one mystical experience
away from a crisis

Music is never loyal

Now I will imagine
pervasive maintenance
hands in a paragraph
reality over time
both getting larger

Logic of experience
soaking up what wrecks

Wax your ballad

Landscape stepping off
a bridge a pleasure
how one tips the land

Funny balloon
floating horrific
talking up the night tree

Parking the car a community
of writers takes flesh
turning inward

How willing are we
to destroy the way out
what surrounds us
is the palace

As though human
lost in the crowd
ignoring his surrender

Buoys and gulls
the rhetoric of inevitability
hits its spot every time

Prom king grill work

Most people on earth
to be conceived
as image

Soulful dogging
digress later

The joker to the joke
there must be an exit

Inkquest requested
no more failure
time is not generous
rainy dark

Up upon night
with Rufus Iscariot
eating meat like
there was a stalking

Giving us audience
entry to the real chain
was to us talking

Sun's appearance
in the anthem
renews the day again

Rage to gas again
against the willing

Reckless skater
swim some more

House of worship
sleeve and patchwork
every so often expectant

Compare notes
with the beaten animal

I amnesia like wildfire
lost like thought
mojo coffin worth entering
raised ground other self

I assume the excess
caused by the hereafter
the higher up of use

Donkey work

Donor captions
I ammunition theft
approving fruition

I done willingly
at hand complete circles
pushing out sleep

Admit the piss
bargained in the raw
in the ascendant

Motherhood rooting
sister sleeping pill
sea bed of night

Louse in the sack
in the cloud havoc

I a moment or two these days
sector breeding
with the objects of mystique

Words taken
away from families

Worlds hover
above us or not at all

Edgy stress of the social reach
love's little kite
what's that swinging

As we now know our medium is
not a making or change
as a parallel I think
you can talk

Rhetorical answers
to actual headlights
in the unbroken slowing
too cold for the animals
to decompose

Moving not the objects
but the rugs beneath them

Method dealer

Augury towers
or how to write
mistakes only

This line imagined
as beneath the feet

How am I like the shark
sleepless and passionate
everyone expecting me

Do not compare
me to the animals

I am nothing like the bear
preposterous
lost to design

There are parts
worth performing
rain to fill our belongings

I am unlike the dogs
caught in the ice
the gaze of protection

Do not capture me
I am not like the horse
approaching the fruit trees
eyes big like fists

I do not wish
to go to college so
I will not go to college

I am nothing like the raccoon
bareheaded in the rain
in the floodlights

Moths in the rose garden
little fawn sleeping
on the side of the road

Love in the roots
in the dead hawk's eyes

I am not like these animals
secretly breathless
with shit in my teeth

Be proof against your will

The casual manner
is competition
revenge yourself
not carefully

Womanhood avenge yourself
horse and carriage
curious pulse

Endearments in
the weapon store
let my people see
on the installment plan

Chimera
acreage

About to get
lost for the night

Never-ending eating place

Mongrel anthem
of known necessity
venture out
count your savings

Honor operator
over my bones

Terror of the peripheral
sleep is not shocking
listening is a ritual
to maintain without pause

Palpable breathing
tiny moments of aging
the mind is spent alone

An orange chair
in the back lot stinking
and soaking up
was it sun or rain

This knowing still exists

Remembrance stood enormous
before its systems
sun I do not
want you on my back

Don't you waste me
weightless exit
everything centers the body

Reflexive lyric lay down the total scale
be careful tonight   sugar
be easy   let's get lazy
in the meadow grass

The real thing bear hug

Here I am
walking into evidence
faces on the waves

Flashlight circle be my guidance
the targets are searching
gathering clues

Full of feeling drafted

For free the spring sentence
baroque technique
deflating shaft of light

Bootleg couplets
jog my weekday

Phrase book watch your step
casual shakedown

Supernatural barometer
of that period and above
mapping untold

Committed to memory
all the rage

Your throat is dry
be the trouble not the balance
glyphic in accordance stoic carols

Tower sniffing

Small bag of the present
at the mercy of the sentence

Here or there the balance
writing out a stage

Weird laughter from
the donkey I wounded

Childhood of my cruelty

Starless valley
who owns this turn

Saw them sleeping
on the carpet
touching upon these things

When can I
be cruel again

Below the window
people in crabgrass

Teaching obedience
to the night train
this tune begging an answer

The answer is velocity
scythe on the front porch
the angle is an answer
beauty begging to be elsewhere

Honey vein police thicket
bring me to thy belonging
and that is where
I can be cruel again

Situation cowboy vortex
witches whistling
amongst peeps

Light in the bowels
my friends you are guilty
can you trouble
yourself to see

Centaur splendor
let me trouble your sight

Read this quickly
you are making
something else

Desire for brethren
was not prompted
accept the light
where no light is due

The affect of our happiness
and so easily supplied
form is evidence
of the lonesome rhythm

Those throats
are thick
with berries

Diamonds are
the tips of her teats

Those dogs in the meadow
are the last dogs
they are looking inward

Unwise visions
surround the pantry

Details in the woodpile
save me from my guessing
harmony's enemies
there at the source

No one birthed me
kingdom carrier
tremors when I launched

Parade nothing

This being my answer
to questions never asked

Who hid this
a bottle in the woodpile
brilliantly shown

The time has come
and talk to these things
a real deer standing
beside a fake one

Red flag totem station

Clean the room
for the hawk

Sleep aesthetic
a loud-mouthed crow
white dogs hanging

Breathless and above
such days faceless neighbor
find the line as follows

Kiss king cough hound

Some beast of feeling
performing birth
as an answer

Upstream Dayton
mercy swallows

The diver to the water
were you waiting

Skinning rabbits
without crying
night is so Colossus

On beyond
back to the rabbits
as the crow flies
back to the hounds

Copy be my witness
wash your lenses
with your phrasing

Straddle channels

A voice uprooted
tape hiss rises
invent the phrase again

Play the tape again
of the waters

Texture trapper
mind your sleep

Purple balloons
in the afternoon
a five-gallon bucket
full of my blue rags

Forever at the crying door
definite shadow doll
jumping to hide

An astronaut's camera
is attached to his chest
joining the weeping
in order to hide

Photo of waterfall
casts shadows

What do you say
of the miles and miles
fish in the barrel
mail-order brides

This reads better in the cold
hiding in the ocean
in a stolen car

Who can hear this
since you care something for me
drunk in the gardens

My blue rags
have some kind of power
smaller than the period
at the end of this sentence

Here is the cabbage
waiting for the troops

Dropping the ringing phone
into the water
all the calm violence
I clearly am missing

Eager retreat

Purr my kitten
your lungs are passionate
barely standing
my pets often return to me

Remembrance
stands before me
parrot phantom
drifting ship

Never healing
little Indians in the systems
a cup of night
I do not remember

Jigsaw cities
ducks in the holler
rabbits in the afterlife
swimming home

Courage circles
beneath the eyes

I have gone
among the animals
with orders to tame them

Cover their mouths
when they begin to sing

It seems to be
at the edge of the question
that kills the body

Is that a washrag
or an animal
my nests in a row

It is on record
the disease covers us
anger at the strip club
sex by memory
is taking you home

Rett has duende

Totem rooster
tasting good

A doubling
in the violence
in the land

Touching upon
apologies for the body
we were all the words again

The perceived
ground and believed

Come and get us officer

Dogs without names

It is in the instead
we find an argument
for the whole

Put this poem
on your shoulder

No more monkeys in the darkness
all's been ground
if all is molasses

Happy banker
where's your daughter

Grasping solitude

What leaves like a flood
comes back like flowers
combing your hair

Do not turn into me

I followed you all summer
falling onto my knees
gathering mud one wants
nothing so much as clarity

This umbrella
does not belong to me

Here is the end
of the dog's rainbow
omniscient and adolescent

Listen to me speak
you who also settle

This is clarity
speaking from Rome

Lucid serpent

His weight talks
and is therefore measured

Spiritual landscape
was replaced
I promised nothing

The literal fragrance
of one's own force

A list of all
the fish in the film
and the stitches which
keep them there

Workable ignorance

Worm out origins
above your head

Scan the magic
your throat is dry

Bend your legs

Do not punish me
young trees stripping
of limbs and bark

Fashion blessings

Sandwiches in the dark

Rhapsody ante
to a degree
in the air unbuttoned

A donkey drowning
in rippled stream
assumes the creep façade

So to speak

Drinking in
an inward man
must be refused

Be possible in nature

A white van
casually crosses
the center line

The deer cats
across the lawn

Revelation is not change
though each of the blossoms
are revealed

Wolf is a verb
horse is

Endless bramble
weakness song
let's get everyone
on the floor

Child the lines
across your body
a bouquet
for our betters

Sleep in our yard
the vowels of heaven
verbal cryptids

Never mind
the eating after

Eggshells in icy water

That which
is accessed by confusion

Private juggling

Who is choosing
joy and essence
unwritten prescriptions
doses taken

Presumed mountain
wears this gown

Polar running

Swine light

Stretching into evidence
this is true ground
hidden in old

Road of excess
palace of Paul

Eat this
and be eaten

Save this and be eaten

Shit coffin hunting
a one-second delay
talking   across an ocean
beneath the plow

Sister saucer
father stump

Hissing public head
and so on meanwhile

Spiral spotting

The image from the beacon
the night's own choired

Compose swimming

Everything you are due
I will soon be sending

Consumed waking

Wash out your mouth
in your heart

Donkey behold

Moving among the binoculars
I do not mean
to be naked before my body

Fish now dwelling
on the table

Boss of my belly

Bastard canons on the loose
cold turkey got me
soon enough

Equals upon the mattress
how can you be sure
the future acre is unwritten

Bat can't bear the instant
assess its sorrows
face to face   songs of praise

Wisp drink

Spawn lightning

Speak your piece
approaching lamb

The nouns are huge
beneath the bottomless lake

Half song of hesitation

Night song of
the soon collected

Absence rooster
eye to eye

Midnight static are you
famous in your city
smashing mountains now

I will decode your race
I have no preference
how to sit for the portrait

Wounds halo hey
here we are selected
weaving not dawning
nestling in a distance

Signature emotions

How can I keep talking
bottles on the tree limbs
a bird in the microwave
self-portrait with
spiders in the grapes

Bypass jackal
singing for his breakfast

That's my anthem

Jelly soften up
a listening contest
how can I keep flexing

Lyric goggles
nothing too shocking
coughing up the right word

Designing the tower a recovery
of phrases takes flight
into acceptance

Here I keep record
of what can be accepted
what the lad has collected
in the balance

Hugely mute, the genius of your legs.

The genius of your legs and the wool lifted.

Another rose from bed like noise.

Time when exterior is mostly hell.

Another rose for witching.

The genius of your legs is not mastered,

no struggle eyeing the instant.

And innocence draped as well.

Tape-loop, a garment mended drop

by drop, another rose doubling.

Another rose, for Orpheus, for being.

Adorned in radiance, a rose.

Severance was clear, was made new

(to make whole). Fiction disappeared

for its veils. Perfection preying.

Another rose of wires. The wind

composed of evenings, parleying.

Notes learned from hearing

the thing that makes. Man

as astronomer, striding among pines.

At unison he arrives, fumbling.

The genius of your legs in endless precision,

unblinking. Day and night working.

Internal organs. Rain drenching.

The genius of your legs on the boat floor.

The nightingale scented with pine.

A week in the weeds. Another rose,

an inner realist. Dusk-sprung accuracies.

The unreleasable and unfinished

genius of your legs. Another rose

melted inside them. Spring came.

Summer came. Ecstatic, another rose

and summer again. Sex as structure,

exchequering. Numinous thorns.

An apostle wrestles with themes.

Mostly bound (to sound) another rose

conceived in violence.

Strangely raised. Verbal pressure.

Begin, being the genius of your legs.

Your legs raised as the very speech.

Genius of our air. A retrieval system.

Speech stores heat, insists on symmetry

seeing the sky whole. Another rose

in the saddle. Loquacious, demonic.

The genius of exile. Exits

as edifice. A thousand wires exist.

Another summer, troubled water.

Another rose in the night-ransom.

Gray magic of blood repeating.

sleep and be there. Spilled
record. Perfumed ruins. Softest tigress
heart of her. Cat's paw
finer grandeur. Sudden heralds above
pound softly vampiric : sun-embroidered, annihilated
serendipitous isolation. Steppingstone. Stasis is
dead (again). Vibrating stabilities. Improvisations
characteristic, periodic. Stranglehold offers form
wolf grief. Hunger. Cucumber. Contemporary
bulge. A swallow. Immigrant sophistication

overemphasis, evidence, milkweed. A bulge
pre-information. Alchemist singing as wolf
and forest. Parallel economies. Characteristic
mimicocracy. Residential dominion, denial. Dead
beast rising. Terrible quotations. Serendipitous
archaeologist. Disappearance : discussion's sliver. Pound
wisdom's tractor. Finger phantoms. Finer
host of a fixed heart
warbler transfixed, nested. Newest record
meant bells, boughs. Scared sleep

wood struck, stacked. Maze meant

evening flourish. Sudden knowledge, warbler

of cause. Small nail : host

riddles before forests. Morning—wisdom's

trade. Partial ancestor, manifested archaeologist

conversational hyperbole; bloodnervous. Easy beast

gifts gently disfigured. Disfiguring mimicocracy

illuminations disfiguring. Loveliest tempest and

sight is blurring listening. Pre-information

off to singing. Twittersong overemphasis

exaggeration parodies focus. Gone off
investigating earliest strata of sight
as stylish audibles, episodic illuminations
imagination prominently erotic. Subject gifts
wounds running, perfected. Operations conversational
simultaneous penetrations co-opted into trade
drama perceived into inward riddles
forth as froth. Haunt of
virtue, pilgrim spirit seeking evening
to sleep in a wood

prone pose through which to
model before notefall, sweeten virtue
in soft flesh put forth
into heaving. Under itself, drama
is motion : becoming, generation. Simultaneous
annunciation. Atrocity translated, gambled wounds
themes dislodged—heroic, oceanic. Imagination
assimilated. Periodic reckoning fissures as
rock, ray. Concerned vibration investigating
strange routes. Precise subvocal exaggeration

sensibility enfolded into wave. Strange
genealogies positing orders. Old rock
of rigor, possible participants assimilated
unanswerable emotional inertia sprouting themes
to forge attraction. Original annunciation
misunderstanding machinery, boundary : Eros is
before surface, after image. Into
such jaws this flew in
notice faces music. Moment's model
still night's, now note prone

call it a nest. Still

revealed : presence. Into knowing's notice

a dog swam with such

support. Water itself released before

a vessel understands inheritance. Misunderstanding's

specificities (uncollected phantasms unleashed to

speech) revised pre-formance. Undervisions unanswerable

elementary. Eternity existed. Yawning of

an age, before direction. Genealogies

of sleep. Dreamdead. Structural sensibility

hallucination, solemnly awake. Scars of
metaphysical intention. Candle lit, an
orb'd realist : eclipsing necessity. Elementary
multiplicity. Identity posited, fancy's speech
sound limits. Repeater : identity's specificities
capabilities atmospheric; perceptive, bitter. A
stabbing desire. Leaning grammar. Support
spark, late taste, sense a
presence within details. Descent revealed
hymns, or the seas, call

soon noon. Come net hymns
stillness stirring. Before, nursing presence
small pool. Breath less spark
eclipse singing—elapse, collapse—stabbing
star. Flowchant, compulsive underpurrings. Capabilities
perpetually speculative, airlifted toward sound
the other listening. Devotional multiplicity
preternatural supermarket. Proportions ever orb'd
train your masters. Resonance. Metaphysical
dusk. Use seduced. Manual hallucination

An emperor's kingdom should not run on common (vulgar) time. In an emperor's kingdom every day is exactly one hour long: the hour lasts from sun-rise to sun-rest. The duration without light, the "hour" of no-time commonly called "night" does not, actually, in an emperor's mind, exist. And so by such rules, in his kingdom, it is also so.

An emperor's sleep is his second kingdom, filled with light. In his first kingdom his subjects adore him. This emperor is one of allowance. The subjects are allowed to run their own labyrinths during the "night" as the emperor sleeps. But even an emperor—even this one—cannot attend to two kingdoms at once.

Each day, riding through the streets, in the holy hour, the emperor enjoys his kingdom, seeing his subjects at leisure. The subjects do not want to disillusion their benevolent ruler and so they engineer a complex means of maintaining the kingdom as he sleeps, alternating shifts of cleaning, constructing, and rebuilding this kingdom which always looks as it should when the emperor rides through, each day, on his fine horse.

The emperor, to gauge the force of his whims, occasionally dismounts and announces to a man, woman, or child some new decree ("we are the currency of Heaven," for instance) and the word spreads and alters when whispered, across the miles. It amuses the emperor as he rides through his kingdom, asking his subjects along the holy route to explain to him the newest decree, nodding with bemusement at each variation. Separate regions of his kingdom adopt different customs and values according to each rumored decree. In the North, for instance, his subjects believe that, as in Heaven, the kingdom's new currency is art.

So now a painting of a horse can be exchanged for an actual horse, a song about a girl may result in the hand of someone's daughter, etc. Some of the subjects of the North begin to spend their nights constructing more elaborate artifices—it works. They grow rich, thick. Predictably, the entire region—and then the kingdom itself—eventually claims no nocturnal professionals or public servants. Systems disintegrate, all the animals again are wild, etc. Art can now only be exchanged for more art. The kingdom disarrays. Starvation. Corruption. Disease.

Terror. The emperor ceases his daily trips and removes himself to his palace, which the shouting subjects now surround, carrying torches. Their footsteps are ever nearer as the emperor, in desperation, composes the story of his kingdom, which becomes, miraculously, his means of buying it back.

AN EMPEROR'S NOSTALGIA

a dozen for Leigh

I.

Future is. Embraceland.

Standing forth, intimate, in an intimate space describing
the apex of the future shape intended.

At night. Points may suggest
a circle as well, engulfed in mist : a mind
if not holy, then in time : intimate : may you and I
offer the other to the gods of attention.

If those up and out accept these offerings.

Beneath the glass floor of a house (ours) are the waters
and all the waters know : the rings.

My actual mind is here too O reminder I am echo (ours).
On the night-bus these thoughts began : darkish bluish blush :
a real house filled with everything I call promise : hello.
To what shall we provide shelter? I place this knot
upon your hand and not upon some promise.

This is the end of terror.

Mercies, and the holy hour is ever near if the word is a stone
which, *in* which, once *in* it, someone finds the gods. Awake.
And the holy hour takes hours I hear : years
or hours of attention, without shelter,
buying, rebuilding the kingdom as it wakes : a walk
built upon the waters. Unwrit hour
where the gods are awake, work complete. Whispers.

Inside the frame a window and below your whispers : the end of terror :

and the word strays, spit unaltered from mouth to moth (to you).

Bewilder'd into memory and not *for* memory :
memory into language
then, not unlike placing a mirror in the waters.

I will extend my gaze—the blaze lays low.

A real house is built again, the daily rooms debugged.
And the living room
will be what? A ghost for which we bleed?
        It is to speak
we drink the animal blood (ours). Books
of this. Jug

jug. I am falling upon our story
of the night

outside the house : it was real. The deaths
                inside a real house

the old woman inside : a sleep
unsound, intimate now with / in herself (the intimacy *too* real
for it is not the one she chose).

For it is squared.

The distance between waking up in this dream
and the dream itself
dreams itself to vanishing. As if
splashed with blood : as though a thigh
smeared our little plane : the very breath.

Enormous eggs we are
silent surplus
and not for the flies.
Not the flies.

We are not for the flies.

II.

Sweet psalmist called motion   aim
  as He is whose whole
Eye no thing is
               cardinals
  and the sweet wide music
sacred suit of each beast
the boast   solemn awe
beholds us extatic
            an orchid
  sews duration   a blessing
for the order   remurmur of
our immense domain   a
  portion of the continual
brilliance pours
           swords
       pouring praise
solace
is your name, sweeter
        than the breath
         of Mary

III.

If the depths are reached after arrives

a long blindness inside which a solitary manifestation

of a mind of some order is psyched : from inside this dream

must we choose? Depths or Heights. Me neither.

Process (here we come) hear us now.

I will put my hands here and there, place here birds

folded out of thicker papers :

out of

because as I've argued they are

in there always / already

in oscillation, between past and, perfection and.

That's where we head. Migration toward

a change in thought, fluttered, the sky

illumine : our illness preps us

for an other Above, one which flies thru, us, here.

I (suddenly I) will discuss you in religious tones :

and shall little birds be in grief for marvels (ours)?

Up on Breeze : for what is isolation

but Song in and not via Wind? We are still in the wind.

We are still in the wind. Same thing (we are in).

Breeze's hidden, moved : much the same. Who here

behind us (here, in the trees) needs no

counterlight refracted, is unaware from what depths

    —from Whose—

each hour comes, to what fine degree each hour

arrives : to string, to bow? As though I mistake each

as my own to refract I carry one thought

(Identities or Things are Neither Cause nor Effect)

toward (They are Eternal) another as a child would,

              from spell to spell.

We are unlike gods so we tend to them →

with a stroke of the chisel.

IV.

Finality goes walking
with the waves. It was mercy
an already spell

and it is a first for me
finally home. Our first form
gold mine psyche

owl heavy with telepathy
mouse skull tapping
antinomian praise

we tend the newest dream
one circle linked with another
mercy. Blood praxis

call of the undoing
heights. Can we hear
the chance operations

equations summoning
precision. A bramble
chain, bumble breeze

contact chanting sense
the assemblage of our scale
is need unleashed

VALENTINE.

Remember a funny night

my family made a circle by and by

like standing on the shore a heart a visceral

thing. This moment my heart's clear.

We'll plant (my heart) a tree here.

My heart my heart my heart.

Is glad.

VI.

Exalting. Paths more precious than gates.
How shall we fill our house?
With paths. Bringeth our wheel over the bones.
Afflicted, clothed? Our
wheel, like a flower forced : into our mouths?
our mothers? Like flowers :
who we face, and how. Stem of a great hour?
Face : you make my heart glad. There the fire?
                    Where no wood is?
My heart *is* glad.
                    Here is the rising.
The laws of kindness.
                            Consider this field.
These candles of our blessings.
                        Bind them to your heart.
My heart *has* obeyed.
                        These aren't dark sayings.
The poison I'm making
is this : love won't lose. You cannot lose to dying
if your case is love.
                        Flight from the earth.
If it helps I have nothing. I'll mention your features
in this book for luck. The arc
of migration and the shape thereafter will be described
by memory : as quick as fish.
The waters below.
            This speech is the stem of the rose
(memory as stem of the act). If we vanquish a memory
let us thereafter wear its skin to ambush
another (I am so happily unaware
I was ever a child among the shadows).
            Our acts may save us.

VII.

Sub-
merged sublime collects :
subdued :
         bodies
are the project

the solitary fawn
               jumps
its delight, sees at a distance a circle
of deer   quiet, low

it is delight
to make an approach

a kiss is a mediation
between forms—into initiation's
                  fuse : grace
carries a body
                over

the fawn's head bows   is subtle
awaits a delight
             it receives

VIII.

Love like consciousness
built with gaps

is certain

what is open is
what gets placed in-between

is here : I have put a portrait of us
in this gap
              a possible whole
sweet nostalgia not to be
destruction but a
              jumping
                      through. So tonight

I am in
my room, in monstrous
  solitude—
                      my ghost
                      has followed you

                              (for comfort?)
as you find yourself
    beyond yourself
weeping

in the farthest room

IX. [Ripple]

totality is impulse
this is our boat, an instrument
defending the private life
our friends, as though words of great magic, sticks and stones
bound toothsomely
when these poems come to life I hope they love us
as though to see, the fire swam
every form imbibes a force
the lilies, the squash, the tomato plants
the news a blue light even in sleep
SUN/SHINE
civilization measured by the light along our walls
all to which we bow in our hours of strength
what wings to bend for a hand
the far swan, as though at sea
as constrained as we are on the limbs of our tree
very attached
a bird conceals its bones, an arrow's hollow sound
and opening all the doors
our bath tonight, a body's oar
these words await our bodies

X.

It accumulates

calla lily   raises a head
inside a beyond
beside us

being signed
ocular spectra blooms   forms
a flowered place
apex of a pyramid

the lilies open
of love, into themselves
day is matrix

circumference for belief
is drawn

holy work of
our hereabouts

our harmony is
the pines

XI.

My god in deep thicket we thought
how much more of us is there.

Not to render the adored but to
render adorable an unimportant world.

Tanglehearted at root we lead each other
to embody some words heft.

In here who answers as we be-
coming dawn draw down like concepts.

Into an inscrutable pouch : water, chatter
to weigh our souls on a feather.

Star riot a pouring down : sky's down
blue as a seed, its philosophy is a rainbow.

Have you seen it lately?

Night all we ask for is under your thumb.
Afternoons of consequence arise in your gyre.

A natural philosophy of skin to touch.
Not to build a house apart or above.

Double fantasia that we matter.
Strangers we are, of this road we are.

Nostalgia.
We become the storm-strum, a branch.

But who wrote our names on the chapel door?
Who built these nests in our necks?

XII.

A breath of sugar (ours)
astonished not to be

a statue or a pale dawn
· a wreath of sugar

the era of great castles
has finally ended

(our architecture
may now be invented)

my chicken this is (we be)
just the tip of the rainbow

A balance in the realism. A balance

is impossible unless it is mistaken in which case let me

count the places   one is discovered

by its sudden presence. A balance is not

totaled as a sum

but instead

measured like love : lips and curves

belong together. A better

border. A bird above the battlefield.

A branch filled with people. A breeze

pushes the canvas.

A century of certain ground.

A certain innocence when I thought maybe

I could come up with a new way to sleep, or to get sleep

out to people (got to get sleep into their lives).

A change of words is more or less

a change of minds. A child killing a bird so

the myth is thickened.

A desire is large, not monolithic.

"*Complex Sleep*" is an index of alphabetically arranged sentences and significant syntactical units (presented in sentence form) that made up a prose poem called *Complex Sleep* which was written between August of 2004 and February of 2005 and was intended as a reconsideration of statements, assumptions and values embedded in previously written pieces. For instance, the sentence "Two swing sets are nearly touching" from my book *Invisible Bride* was rewritten in *Complex Sleep* as "Two sentences are nearly touching." Most of the sentences, however, diverged much more distinctly from the seed sentence or line. The line "warbler transfixed, nested. Newest record" from the poem "Ink Drop," for instance, was rewritten as "Warbler, all the lilies have wilted."

This index was arranged in its current ordering on the evening of February 28, 2005. A further restaging occurred in the last week of July 2005 as line breaks and spaces were inserted into the piece.

A different person wrote
the same thing.
A dreamed control / specifics
dancing / on whose grave / the children as brides,
as always / fire is a fine way to argue (the emotions
need to be specific). A dying form knows
that not everything translucent
is transcendent. A face
like leaves is languaged in the act.
A fact has its own topology
(the joy of not knowing).
A finger has an eye and an ear and
other openings. A footnote alerts, alters a singing : is gracenote,

gravity : significant :

an available scream.
A happy child steps out
of the wreckage (lucky scars) to become like us brushed with blood.
A hex on how the other half lives.
A highly advertised reversal :
an unfrozen perfection. A hole in your body

where this poem wanted to be.

A knife in the sun.
A language which lets me write as I sleep :
as in most fictions we are both situated in relative repose.
A list of realities.   A long awaited rain darkens the door, floods

several childhoods.

A looking seasoned to taste. A make-me-new, make-it-now

desperation.

A newness calling one sea. A night spent sweating,
punctuated discussions of discursive traps.
A nose can grow to be monstrous : how many photographs

are published to make this point alone? A nurse

for these greetings. A pattern

of desperation is sketched and then painted over so

             it will then be appreciated.

       A pleasure rose, from the ashes.

       A private consciousness constructed from public discourse

             is an Eros built from errors.

A retrieval system

for that? A root as though

    the tree knew how it ended

           but kept speaking (like a hypnotist) in the dark

             that was offered for speech.

A root exposed of the last volume.

A sausage party.

             A sentence I can deal with :

             the predetermined areas

             expand into something beyond a beyond.

  A sentence or two descended from birds

  I am speaking in tones.

     A shift of consciousness into the sentence itself

     is possible (writing the sentence, one

     becomes the sentence). A simple desire

     to ride a horse across America.

A spotted fawn with one eye missing. A story

built by heart. A subway

filled with insects, begetting history.

A trace of annihilation in the reflection

    —sunburst—

           more reflection.

    A trace (sheer

    pleasure) of melody before the sentence.

A value is therefore found

in an individual's retreat from individualism

and idiosyncratic movements. A vision

from the porch. A vision is

also a place (it is found, claimed and defended).

A voice in the body

drowns a voice in the mind. A voice

invested with power makes me white with desire. A wiener dog

on the way home (judging the dead) eating a possum.

Above all

I was responsible for you.

Across the way is rain, foppery.

Adorned prose wedded

to the head streaming. Aeon is

as an open system opposed to the flood.

All the paper authors

backlit by a sky. All the students

are back on campus today.

All theories are safe, in retrospect.

Although my cradle was burned hours ago

I still am asleep. An anger

mixed into the track for now.

An ant   at the windowsill

meditates,   a witness.

An apostle wrestles with the message : themes age

beneath labors.

An archaic ship appeared before us—magnificent—we tore it apart

to understand the code.

An elaborate trajectory best taken by a simple craft :

condense understanding. An idea

is introduced to magic. An image grows indeterminate :

is there a bird beneath his feet because he's transcendent or is he
just cruel?
Analogous structures are now being sought.
And a first light that holds now in stillness :
it was said to illuminate an eternity.
And I know enough
to act naïve about the light in the earth, the faces of death.
And I who struggles to place his tongue on your eye
have seen this sentence before
between solar and lunar moods.
And if one can hear music pushed back by the gods one should
understand all by good.
And it was the memory of
the prayer hall and intricate engravings that finally
saved me. And once we entered Bel-Air
our whole lives were before us, superfluous
(but not absurd).
And the color grid sings
"do renew your dues—unless do you approve of our abuse."
And the phantom they built was a container for history.
And the repetitions of my day are heartening evidence.
And the swords on the wall will have to be used.
And unless the words revise us we cannot survive.
And we who sleep smoothly in our darker hemispheres
without wonder?
And what else could they do. And what recurrent sighing
is in our capacity, what whimsical perspectives? Anger forms a focus
teasing our limits. Animals
of a possible intellect.
Annunciation without appointment.
Another egg we stole from the dragon as it was sleeping.

68

Another heart inside the horse's mouth : relax your mind.
Another magnitude to dip into / to trim / it fits the shadow
(body of light).
Another monologue.
Another path of directness is achieved :
both faces merge in the image of the missing eye : achieved : love's
organ's absence
allowing both of us to be seen.
Another sentence flourishes as defined.   Another song of
joineries : lower lip,
upper lip : two sides,
a soft coin.
Ant, are you
into what I am into,
an opposite of first sight?
Archaeologist, all the knowing is overheard
(overhead). Are you still going to let me define you?
Around the bend are thousands of crow-lined tile-roof houses,
drawers full of letters.
As alarums resound ideas are approached.
As I adjust (this is just for the fun of it) for the fawn outfit
there is stirring singing even as the carcass writhes :
the gaze gathers.
As I pulled out she heard a chanting.
As I stiffened in the down I grew imprecise pretending to be entire
in the middle of nowhere.
As I was childless and alone I sought to lay with the world
and endow it with small works.
As one joins Homer and Whitman roaring in the pines one makes
a decision on value.
As one writes out   all-one-is-not

one writes out   that-which-one-shall-eventually-be.

As the night begins your lips produce smooth stones at first sight :

perfection gained

grain by grin.

As the snake struck at my heel

I fell into trance, wishing in and out for sleep.

As these are the surrounding texts they make me sand.

As though the word had corrupted the entire world.

As we go up   we go on

to announce the death of discourse.

Asleep at midtown, in a velvet chair :

a boundary was reached.

Assimilated into the design closure becomes good news

disappearing and coalescing amongst efficient minds.

At last we are united.

At midnight we are complicit

with the appearance of things.

Away from bed we were even shier.

Back in *Ulysses*   is art. Back

to the equation. Backyard

lyricism. Be lingered upon and subtle

in the mirror. Be patient,

soup. Be weary with me of the sentence that senses enough has been
said.

Beak of wisdom, feather of faith.

Because the accidents are arranged they are an extension of power
(classically trained).

Because of the persistence of the theme upon the psyche

moving objects are multiplied, deformed.

Beast who has come to be returned has come to be denied :
exhaustion ritualized.

Beds are made, sleep occurs.

Before, the body had eyes.

Before the city uttered or was quoted by

riots : I walked onto the plane under the shrill moon, pierced and

glad,

demanding some sort of victory

(I felt sad as I saw the fires below).

Begin now, being in, be gun : being will travel

(I just want to see your face).

Behind every successful man stands a canonical index singing truth.

Blind children who learn to

imagine their losses.

Blue yodel (please

come in and out of the rain).

Books or mice beneath the couch. Bring the fish home

I wish to kiss all of you on your mouths.

Brought to the glaze that we had paid for, we waited.

Bugs that whisper in our ear.

Bulge at the business end of the three-headed dog.

But all along our watching the landscape became an answer to

memory,

delicately scratched by the

frame.

But I have no sorrow.

But one also tends to define one's self by avoiding the definitions

offered

by the self and others

as friendly or enemy fire. By my brother's name I say

decision is the soul.

By over-quoting my sources I have revealed only myself.

By the time I get into your daydream it is

swarm upon swarm. Call and response

of your extremist wing. Cantos

beyond mercy.

Capabilities, soft surrealisms and basic human desires

are also strong in here.

Characteristic explanation, "there is no present

except the one demanded by your histories."

Clean contentment in that I have never feared for my life.

Cobweb catches

a dying leaf.

Complete evasion and me

down on the bayou.

Composed from the vantage point of paradise :

sitting chilly with fear in the cone of light.

Composed we are pleased to look for words. Composition is

concentration :

exaggerated.

Conceived in fiction.

Continually let us hit the future so it knows we're there.

Conversational, the officer's intelligence

allowed nature in : we drove home, fully aware.

Countries of respective wings thrashing themselves

to prominence. Cursed by your curves I will risk definition.

Cut as we are (from a secondary cloth).

Dark days

(the eye withers).

Dave you left your seed in their mouths.

Dead in the dream boat

he rose. Dead there is

nothing inevitable. Destruction is

a king of discipline.

Dim delight in change;
however fine, however blind. Dissecting guesswork
one is forced to inscribe it.
Distorted because of the source and not because of the transfer.
Do you claim to know the Jews now that you recognize their beards?
Do you feel that you know me
now that I've revealed this sentence to you?
Drag of air.
Dragged forth into portraiture a sequence of seizures is distinct
from the spells involved.
Drama is a form of sincerity :   serious praise for time and space.
Dressed alike
the dead man and I make eye contact for a solemn hour.
Drift down, cricket.
Drop
by drop.
Drugs
present themselves : offerings, zoologies. Drunk
on the conclusion which is dawn.
Each person thoughtfully placed
to consciously comment on every other person.
Eclipse
cumulative. Elementary relatives play their role,
air for the sentence.
Enough about the momentum of truth.
Esoterica strokes his retina.
Eternal bass lines.
Evening now and the storm is, as anticipated, a drainage of power.
Event we wore for the world to peer through.
Eventually the impossible is proven false
by familiar words.

Every month

I think of my family for a solid hour,

of smallness facing the world.

Everyone knows Duchamp was nothing other than

a mile of string.

Exactly wrong the surface was instantly recognizable.

Exaggeration at this point would only be an aesthetic affirmation

of the current regime. Fair descent

into birth. Filled with pills

(let the rewiring be good).　　Finer yet : explain these things to the

hangman.

For all my life the clouds flying overhead like daguerreotypes

(like making believe).

For hours I am Sleep King seeking an unfolding and unlocking

within a commingling.

For I have certain fears I must project an imperial muse.

For instance

I desired to test the tolerances of my body—shorter breaths, quicker

thoughts—

though I did not keep a record. For me

the challenge was as I saw it

to reveal as mere sentences

that which I thought I had become.

For now anecdotes of self-preservation are of a higher priority

than those of flagrance or asylum

or of faith.

For you have neither a humanistic nor formal approach to linguistic

value

you are damned to drift into major streams. For us

punctuation is a kind of sculpture. For we know our true spirit is slow

O Lord (let us aim our selves

[at his abeyance]
as we are His weapons). Form of the future :

                                 clowns who look the roses in the eye.
    Forth as froth : whether in or out of sleep

                                 I lust for the flexible,
the feline, the cinema
of the anemic. Game of verbs in circulation
at every point of the sentence, in varying degrees of dominance

                                 and control.
Genealogies checking themselves in exodus, "enacted through the

                                 flesh."
Genius either does or does not draw its next sketch
        from the white spaces mapped out by the previous ones :
waters from an evident well. Genius of an other

                        (you can't refuse). Gifts :
general drunkenness, a rope, the living drone, a crushing landscape,

                             mother on the phone.
Gnats between the window and the screen,
        damned birth.   God of the plough.   Grace is
    the biggest departure. Gray days of easy agreements. Grief

                             graph. Grief is
internal in nature, a mental exercise. Hallucination is
interesting in my manner :

                    because of these exaggerations
                    more subtle truths
                    may be detected and finally tracked down.
Hawks of some kind

                             on the swaying treetops
and a small animal
of some sort

                    here with me beneath the house.

He is to what he speaks

as a savage is to the ages : true, beautiful, and good.

He who is false still functions.

Heart played

victoriously in a visible Hell . . .

added to creation . . .   do not forsake me.

Heating the spaces to be stepped into. Here comes

the morning orange.

Here in America free from the freight   some of us are blinded by

answers.

Hiding beneath the bed we find that communication consists

of making a face

and then holding it for hours.

Hijack this thread.

His whimpers were an element of the design. History lessens

(great works and surprising moments aside).

Home is on the line (sing it). Host unfamiliar,

the quiet whispering is writing a book

I cannot stand.

Hours at rest in the washroom, hands and knees,

refining the senses. How to enter the lucid epoch?

However love will wash the mind with sight.

Hugely moving (we were

hugging all the Japs).

Hymns for lining and prayer : if you do not understand the words

please do not moan along. I a bestial intellect can only

lead us away from the flood or carry us through :

no prescriptions or descriptions from me.

I am a drunkard in the gathering gaze.

I am a little high strung myself, sounding a note

when the wind hits.

I am an ideological necessity : according to such and such a set of
circumstances
the poem can no longer justify its existence   *ergo* it should have
died
ergo it is dead
ergo it is death
ergo it is me. I am an obituary :
a site where dying is reported and performed. I am entirely
unconvinced
by this art walk. I am going to be the best part of this feeling
that we're not trying to manage the afterlife
but letting it happen all by itself. I am produced. I am too old for
experiments.
I an attack upon art have become art myself :
flop,   flop,   flop.
I can smell the bullets.
I cannot get away from the possibility of this or that image (the dog
has eyes).
I cannot let you think what you see. I cannot sing and yet I love.
I change the wording in order to protect her. I couldn't see for the
glory of the light.
I don't want to be discouraging
(my line
breaks
like a little girl).
I end up. (I fell in love with trees
and that's when I grew leaves.)
I have found the above miraculous.
I have in fact wholly detached myself from everything :
a corrective crystallization :

I'm very attached to this sentence.   (I have laid aside my male attire

for you.)

I have pointed my TV at your ceiling. I have seen an end to

perfection.

I have tamed lions by strangling my love. I know.

I know how these things are born here (in the afterlife). I make

myself monster enough

to engulf it. I put sheets of paper all over that mountain. I

recognize

that not all sensations are immediate.

I saw your scarf flutter. I the one lost in beginnings am a meal

among men.

I told you about swans upon swans / you know the place / where the

nothing is / real.

I too timid to reside only in change recognize that in this world

(as in Newton's) if all the things were emptied from the sentence

then the sentence would disappear (with the things).

I use the idea a couple of minutes later.

I who mouthed an entire body am even now pretending to change.

I will add this

to the way. I will allow this fact

to become currency, a token of exchange.

I will not allow you to write on it.

I will not read my new poem in public. I would like to set up a few

fetishistic patterns here

in order to create a sense of either obsession or

suppression.

If anything can get into the sentence then nothing can.

If I am still a beast at nightfall we will know that nothing has

changed.

If in doubt pound it out.   (If the past is prologue

how much does it matter that I fathered two children
before I turned sixteen?)
If this is correct then my body must eventually reject its
organizations.
If you are Charles Olson, robed and bundled, tell me :
is this why I need to survive?
If you are frightened
by the way I (with such ease) erase one world and then utter its
replacement
then please join me tonight : gathering in the shadows. If youthful
and lovely
then spilling with terror.
Illuminations weakening by degrees :
I'm getting by on winding resolutions (sharply remastered).
I'm troubled by the young, their terrifying poses
(dancing on the screen).
Imagination disciplining the state, allowing it to blot out at work
the sun
with its body an agent of practical value and not just of uprising.
Impossible
to form a false picture. In bed we watch—we forget to move—and
wait.
In the text it is as if the flesh sings and you can take that
as my error.
In Egypt and my blanket is miles away. In here
they let you breathe the oxygen
of publicity. In love all is one tongue.
In my body is some thing imaginary. In my hour of deliberation
the ventilator turned off and on; this was like sleep : desirable.
In my transparencies, an aim at instruction.

In the evening I am kneeling before your body in apology. In the field
of green inkling

he was tapping for hours. In the idea of a consistent body there are
lesions :
if such body-stable (centered) idealism is rejected it isn't to deny
bodies or centers or even stables
but to allow them to be newly discovered throughout the night.

In the idea of beauty there are at least five lies :
one is escape.

In the moral struggle between nations of beauty there is precise
trembling.

In the sentence nothing is incidental but in the world
sentences certainly are.

In this circle we will hold hands as I recite the history of our
line.

In this manner I am entered from behind.

In this present state my interest in dance
lies only in that sometimes I find myself having been a dance :
when an idea is given one is lashed to it.

In this wind I feel nothing but a breeze

and talons.

In time let me sell these discrete sentences as a single unit.

Individuals are cast
in comedies : these fictions do not leave them disemboweled as often
as asleep

but the potential is there (in the sentence).

Inner rhetoric
here. Inner traps are

set for exterior predators.

Intention is a limitation and a happiness.

Internal dialogues brought to dance-sing on demand, disconnected
(we are peeled) from feeling.
Into the heartland my hours descended.
Investigating the noise I discovered that it was
in fact a picture (possibly
in color) that had been framed and nailed to my wall.
Is the south rising again tonight
through its turnstiles?
Is this / my new poem the projection / a radically descriptive
program. Is this still a question.
Is this then your vehicle in our driveway? It being a means
of teaching others how to sleep. It glows.
It has rather the character of a colorful flower that eats bugs. It is
a familiar thought :
this afternoon is worth keeping because of my close attention
to particulars
and because of the visions—deep, dependent, late—made possible
by my endless compromising.
It is necessary for the heart to suffer
the confusing grotesqueries of a large idea.
It is necessary that one be perfectly situated
so that one can be shaken enough to empty one's self
to completeness. It reminds me of the days when we were all
unknown. It was me
the entire time.
It's of interest only to the extent that it becomes itself (its elf).
It's the strum
of passion and definition, a local chord.
Its tradition not so much inherited as purchased.
Its vanishing points indefinite and sincere
my new poem defines the world in two terms.

I've been casual before the camera in positions of compromise

(standing, running, kneeling). Knew we were in the flow

early on : bees stinging, spit hanging, agape

at the making.

Large particulars also agitate the waters. Left alone the night
has eyes,

the blind have eyes. Let it breathe.

Let me introduce to you

a man conceived in violence and raised by strangers. Like Pavlov

one is astonished to find salvation

where there is no physical cause for it.

Like the fat men in your memories there are agilities here but only in
the extremities.

Like the otherness of this crowd you are judging my past

phrase by phrase

(thank you).

Like this

my portrait is the proliferation of my ego by new means, in a new
mode—

an eraser is another instrument (but the contours, the shapes).

Look alive. Looking back

it was we who disappeared. Love is accorded its fury.

Low reflection, let me speak from my ignorance. Lyric as such

has placed its bets on me. Meant "river," said "river."

Melted—just so.

Metaphysical, I fell like this, into the well. Mimicocracy

of the old school building

a better tomorrow without cessation.

Misunderstanding my negotiations as narratives

my family applauded

the bottom line. Model airplane and a kite

on the unmade bed.

Morality should be a by-product

and not an end in and of itself. Mortality

       should be easy.

    Most of the day I am trying to create my own shadow

        and at night inventing methods for making it disappear.

    Mostly he wanted music to be his master

like light. Multiplicity of brotherly love.

      My adolescence was a question of class affiliations

        continually attacking each other.

My backing away is an erotic gesture (madness reveals methods).

    My changes are exchanged for value.

    My emblematic identity is intact.

   My escape in an image's better manner, accomplished in flames.

      My eye recalls a knight

   being pinned to his horse by an arrow that passed through both

            armored thighs

   (with the horse and saddle between). My head a sex hat,

my face blackened : unwanted understanding. My life

          as a cog.

My life as a door. My lips are moving

   I must be thinking.   My mornings are strange

       and no one's to blame.

My one pure image mowing beneath the willows.

    My problems arouse me :

   the flowerings infected, steadily giving forth : hysterical.

    My voice invades a new text

and comes back squealing. My whole project

depends on my ability to say things. Myth

      as meth.

       Myth

sick. Nature

has placed spiders in my sheets.

No decentering occurs outside my frame.

No more broken wing. No one can rise to prominence like this

nonce by nonce. No reason to leave this room (except perhaps

the driving range).

No role is too old : what

would we have said in other worlds?

Not a new sound but

a no sound. Not just emotional

but strategic. Not

straying from the original

but playing it with different instruments.

Not that we wanted in the storm so much as

we wanted to be

at home. Notes

accumulate in nature for they, like us, are perfected forms.

Notes the man :

"this sentence did not exist an hour ago but an exactly similar

one did."

Notes shrunk. Notice face's music, asleep

in dead laws. Nouns offered as perceived differences,

opportunities

for perception :

diagrams, valentines. Of all the available options

I choose story. Of course

mirrored beyond belief. Of course

the attacks changed everything no matter how low key you are.

Of my genealogy I know this :

there are chairs arranged throughout the acres, released.

Of my past I know

it is time to scrape the shit from my shoes. Of symmetry
I know a cluttered night with a white flag lifting, and
correspondence.

    Of this wall of sound I am only a soft percussion.

        Off in the minutes : an arabesque

                around which the children gathered

                carrying blood. On my egg

                are cracks, specks :

                common roots.

    On the back of my neck are lesions and burns—

        these are elements of the design (the difference is

                        spreading).

On thinkable ground presume this much
(these small colored stones).
One can only know so many things

                    (stay away from Little Rock girls).

    One continuum

presents a slinger whose shot arrives so sweetly it feels like a kiss.
One hunts among eggs.

           One stands on the side of the road,

        head bleeding, "hunting for Croatia."

One starts with the sentimental, the couple in the next room—

        their sounds sketching a kind of beyond.

One theme succeeds another like generations within the spaces

                  through which we run.

        One writes one's shadow

                but not with one's hand.

Only it makes me stronger. Or the simplest system. Orb'd
in to a shadowed unity dispersed throughout its showing

        a final period is an error : its lone invention. Ordering of

                hands, of lilies.

Ours is a nation of stable forms. Out here

                       simplistic notions of truth are useful.

Outlaws are at home in the storm.

       Outside the bathroom window one evening I watched a tiny

green frog

                  wake up on a stalk.

Overemphasis cohering into a consistent perspective.

       Overhaul.

Paramnesia is my other tonight.   Perpetually now my central

loyalties

          are made partial, combed down.   Phantoms

              as though philosophical points.   Pigeons

              have nothing to do with this sentence

                and this sentence

              has nothing to do with pigeons.

                            Please

              be faithful in New Orleans.

              Pleasure crews.   Plus this

            (pulse this).   Poems conceived in violence.

                            Poems

      dragged like corpses along the shore.

              Ponds shaped like a bird's head.

              Poor spiders in the rain.

                            Pound

                  one's heritage :

                    weigh it : color it

                    in and out.

Pre-information progresses downward into objective data

       (just passing through). Presence disappoints, mowing alone,

                      pulling away from the waters.

Production without participation, the miracles of chance : a mirror is
still a mirror.

   Prone and desirable my wife was there, a nice figure on the
unmade bed.

      Rain is interesting despite its banality or maybe because of it : an
                                                      indoor life,
a fidelity to the movement. Record of complexity I never asked for
the truth.

         Revealed : my determination is simple and settled :
   I am no longer your child climbing onto a goat's back. Riddles
signify

               interruption, the misplacing of keys.

               Rock in hand I contemplate

                  a past (a window

               in the shape of a serpent) too intimate to forgive,
                  an agent of theft and release.

   Roof finished but we still don't like the rain.   Satisfaction is
                                             obstruction.

   Screwed at the center and the circumference.
Secondary peaks are scaled in vanity—
one ripples the wind with surfaces,

                  the emotions aligned.

         (See the image of a swan raping the waters
   in my newest book, *Mt. Cleverest*, forthcoming from Flood Editions.)
Seeding night minds via the blood (we are nonabsorbing) beneath
these feet.

            Seeing the old man quote himself in the interview
   I allowed myself to assume that that's not what it means to be
human :

                        it was me the entire time.

Sensibility like a saint, marching through. Sentences, deliver this news.

Sentences that are found to make release possible.
Serendipitous world shadow : you are a moving picture,
an imbalance of light accomplished by that full fleeing of an other
whom we designate as missing.
Severance without a way, without an objective. Shall we gather
always like this,
leaves in a river? She gets to be meticulous this morning—the heat binds me.

She is now open to pleasure.
She makes out without us. She makes up
her wake up. She rammed her mind into memory
and gripped the wheel.
She was of a spirit so human we must wonder at her control.
She wonders if this is fear. Sheets curled up like letters,
written like song.
Shit like this is real; a death rattle, a death threat. Shoulders open,
mouth heaving. Sight follows motion (mention).
Simultaneous and unsolicited, my submission to you is complete.
Sleep must be seen from this distance if one is to possess
a sense of its terror (as it has been fixed).
Sleep on the sentence (sleep on the roof). Small mall
dissolving. So let the sea wax mad.
So the lecture
begins. So then do we
recognize ourselves as everything we cannot see.
Some girls. Some mornings
the fawn enters the yard and even though
the animal turns its entire body in order to see
I cannot think with violence.

Some nights dryly shadows are possibilities not necessarily stressed.
   Something else will have to keep this going.

                           Soon enough exploit the healing.
Sound of one tribe clapping. Space again : this is the place
    to map the route we were. Spark persistent enough in its vision,
rising.
Speaking as a sacrificial eating, staged and bleeding. Speaks to the
shapes for us.

      Specificities of the best of times. Speech
        has always developed well along coastlines, in rebuttal.
    Speech is my spinach. Spring sympathy. Stabbing
    the star did you   put on airs, insisting as you do
                      on notions of form?
Star marked by interior textures, coats filling a room, garden gone to
                    seed : bad moves.
   Static as an answer to abundance : the known is the constant
change.
    Still, the sun god must be united with something other than
skin.
  Stillness on the phone, tell me how
    love is succeeding. Stirred sentences,
  who planted you ("Johnny Appleseed") one after another
    so he'd have a path back home? Strange then
              this repose, a trick of the trade.
  Strangely the pivot can be used
    regardless of material. Stuck in the back
      with the noodles. Such small gestures make
   reception memorable. Summer sum : the year is conducted
    as the tides are (it is cheated—just so) : summer is or isn't
          a pause in the dream.
Support so the first writing is a complex writing.

Suspended objects are blue in the green light.

Taking my time calling you back

I didn't know I was adding to sorrow.

Tape-loop tell me : is this wisdom, is that madness : what is in
your jelly roll?

Tell me who you will believe. That was me

a myth among the members.

That woman who walks in here every afternoon but always as a
different man

is crying again. The actuality

overwhelms the egg

(I guard my master's egg)

as we feed each other.

The adult movies are great but too many people

die while making them

(this is just one of my acquired convictions).

The animals line my skull.

The attack will be against the institutionality of art : not that
it is artificial :

against official notions of cause and effect : not that they are
untrue

(this is just to say that in retrospect it will make for good analysis).
The body is potentially explosive; we have visions,

we have bodily perceptions.

The boomerang

returns.

The bottle is most of the story

but little of the message.

The crossing they sell has sails. The cure for space
is vision. The dead animals line my study. The detachment

as of now is finished :

the smoke and blood no longer linger.
The difference between thinking clearly and confusion
is never the same.
The different phrases
of the moon; only reflections.
The distance between what is cooked and
what one hopes one is cooking.
The distance is too small, the details too obscure,
the pinnacle lingered upon
too exactly : relax the bow.
The example of Cubism has been of no use : trees
have weight and not just bark.
The eye is not involved in memory; that's our glory.
The fact is one doesn't consider the sex good
unless the bed ends up at least two feet away from the wall
(hatred can keep
a man alive).
The fact that orchids can grow
high in the branches of the rain forest, that they have aerial roots.
The far-off
gets in your face like a hand tracing shadows.
The fashioned and the executed are within.
The father ejaculating on the mother.
The film is everywhere.
The future was a shadow to kick around :
a lot of dream imagery. The heart of our works is dust, a
green bird in a cat's mouth. The heart
tells us not to speak perfection.
The hill of ice spreads and we both suddenly realize
how little value we hold for fragments.
The immediate wake. The ink froze (put it in the boat).

The instant I found myself conscious of the absence
of sensory input from the external world I on empirical ground
concluded

that I was asleep.
The invitation is terrifying, dancing on the screen.
The jellylike substance in which one is embedded.
The laughing tongue, the speech act. The light in other words is a
metaphor
(sleep with the light). The limitations of vision are what allow sight :
through this window, with this screen. The lion says
"my monstrosity—my lack and mastery—did this to me."
The lion smiles tonight (let sleep melt within us). The lips that lisp.
The lobster escaped us and dwelled happily in the distance.
The long life has eyes. The lovely details accumulate about us.
"The lyricist and the activist are singing the same song . . ."
The man with an accomplished sense of smell measures things off
in the blackness,
stands stillness.
The men are working becoming the street.
The misuse of experience will guide us to new jetties.
The mountain meows. The next sentence will not oppose
institutional poetry
but instead carry it forward until it collapses of exhaustion in
the middle of town.
The night looks like circles.
The objects of understanding (more precisely the shades) like
little green leaves
just conceived.
The only arena of communication here is physical space.
The original design was an outpouring, a little
connector : let me pick up your hand.

The pacing and phrasing of major emotions; cerebral conductors.

The past

is produce.

The perfection of verbs

as a fulcrum of being. The pines,

the sleeping sticks.

The poem was finally finished and that was when we wept

(we went into the upper air).

The point of drugs is to feel nothing.

The pretty things are here again

(bent by details).

The previous sentence was an absolute failure,

one that this sentence can only pretend to live up to.

The pulse of a body

mentioning its presence into its own ear :

a body undressed : washed and judged by the mind.

The question was

when to enter the class that had conceived me to destroy it.

The real value is in learning to be wrong in the process

while still being right there. The rhythm

of disappointment. The scene, for the seer, is further proof

of his or her will.

The sentence is interested only in the durations of experience

which produce sentences.

The short live

short lives.   The sign dilates. The sleep

that chases my mind teases me with duration

(the music and the musician aligned against me).

The sleepers are very shy and remain untouched. The soil is

being raised

(and not by recollection). The sound my one pure image makes
is meaning.

    The sun is wet.

      The sun is nothing outside of its context.
(The swan

was Paul.) The thorns are not only on the head but of the heart.

    The torch showed us where the animals were sleeping.

    The transition of light to language is created

      in each person shaping him or herself in the shadows.
The trees go all the way

    down to the ground. The trick is to keep treading

        even as the spirit hangs.
The value is absolute and can be calculated :

  put the devil in his Hell and close the oven door.

      The vehicle ridden

      bears no resemblance to understanding.
The waters that we actually drink.

      Themes are never emotionless before our eyes

        but continuously appear and disappear.
Themes skillfully acknowledged I erase my brother as a furnace from
the page.
Then the image is driven repeatedly inward.

    Then the monolith floats away and we begin to copy it.

    Then there are no depths without flowers :

      there is a deception of lowers (this speaks my language).
Then we stop being reasonable. There are trees swaying before me

        lit from within.
There I found myself melancholy on light ground.

    There in the many inches of sleep is a capability of elaboration :

  at last we enter a space that allows for something other than
function :

every cell of a body alas has its function.
There in the street I pronounced myself dead so I was allowed back in
the club.

There is a screen available for our buoyancies.
There is betrayal at work, carefully haunted. There is honor
in bending to time.

There is something primitive about an animal.

There was finally
an absolute whole available in variations forever contorted
(dear repetition) into the greatest impregnable simplicity.

There was never an everlasting.
There's a man cutting open a thing : a gift of material, an
allowance of time
for the pose (like Picasso hold the light). These days
I'm practically writing the spaces between words. These days
we are faster
than our future. These vibrations were solidly assumed
and we were not unlike heaven ourselves : rotating, slipped away.

They are playing with our emotions
but we are playing for keeps. They're superstitious
down at the supermarket (lacking belief for all the wrong reasons)
caught as they are in your web.
Thinking is more useful than knowing (but less useful than sleep).
This does rely upon an acceptance of the body : a consideration of
decomposition . . .
of proportion's
responsiveness.
This is for my children when I am real.
This morning after sleep we took turns taking showers.
This thing we have continually labeled dream
is actually a property of something very familiar

(a symptom of waking). Thus I am like a woman
        and need these things explained to me.
    Thus we fall in love all over again. Time slowed
by actual hands. To be more exact
        grief can be considered an instance of dreaming
                constrained by sensory inputs one wishes to avoid.
    To forge a new vision is to elevate the paper into an old dialogue.
            To forget the scene
            he built a fawn out of words.
To leap underground. To make it known who will let it free
(let nature bee).
    To move a greater distance within a sentence than most
paragraphs allow.
            To move to the south, to go to college, become a tycoon, retire
                and then become a rock and roll star.
    To prefer always the living is to favor a tree simply because
    it is on this side of the river. To present fine things to your wife
                on your way down is standard.
                    To shame one's friends into emotion.
To sing more like a dog or more like an egg. To sky is not to wander or
lord over
        but to blend cunningly (O Lord) the one and the many.
    To this sleep work is calling. To this your body we have brought our
                    own methods.

        (To what song has this sleeping slipped?)
Tone of your valley

                            (lay down in your valley).
    Trace the following down, pulling it on,
putting on airs. Tracing backwards : the landscape as the road
describes it.

Tracks are here for the scope, images for a beautiful and
imported sleep.

Trade routes are traditional channels of cultural transmission,
erogenous zones where stances of submission and domination are
developed.

True belief is singing seeing.

Two by two we slip into the woods (flames seek degrees of
affinity).

Two sentences are nearly touching.

Unanswerable : the phrase

has eyes. Unblinking I drive

my feminine pulse to a beat surrender.

Undulates in ways we expect.

Unsketched and completely finished

they are never more than an inch or two away. Utterance-game

I am strictly roots.

Virtue is always understated (isn't it?

isn't it?). Warbler, all the lilies have wilted.

Water for the crossing.

We are beginning to believe in torture

as an effective process that produces real results.

We are little,

in the ladle.

We can build a museum out of any catastrophe.

We could no longer hear the sound of the bath water

("in actuality the roar of the dream sea").

Well, yes : we all reside in a weird displacement.

What can I offer in equivalence?

What is the writing up there, thrown forth in a palsy,

the limousines waiting out in the street?

What paths / what to burn / to show

the self as present / presence.

What to pierce, when to pin

possibilities of meaning when the real men say

she has valorized virtual memory over the actual mind

(in the sex act?)?

Whatever we can believe we can also have replaced

(looking at the canon

one becomes the canon) (logos apprehended

as spirit). When I feed my cow the buzzards come.

When I wrote a revolutionary sentence

I got so excited—often I would remove my glasses

and study the sentence for hours

and then I'd open the window

and start shooting my gun.

When love succeeds

it is impressive.

When one meets a mentor one enters the change.

When they dragged my body over the statue's face

I understood : the crickets heard us.

When we wake we find that nothing has changed.

Where can I insert

my language?

Where there is song there's order : "all our lives" we sing

"all our lives."

Why are they using paint to persuade us

that we sprouted forth from the earth?

Will,

hold the leaf to the branch; a wind will carry the message.

Will this

green annihilation spread to us and our present value?

Wind is

wept.

Wisdom's portrait is apparently finished.

Wolf I raised

why do you get like you do?

Words / let me be / your monster.

Words were

never the truth.

Wounds marked by interior textures,

meat on the scales.

Yes it is time to swallow certain words.

You are quiet as we dim the lights

and creep into the meadow where the small deer feed.

You walk out of one room and into another. Your act is a first act

separating light from darkness.

Your brother asks me to describe

the demands of silence.

Your denials have traveled far and still look forward.

Your flow

is fly.

Your head was taken

and perfected.

It heals to not pull blood in

poor silt as it sinks at the foot of a sea

It does not skip off the page

a real dream that does not give us skin

and yet grafts to a neck or head

roof off, sky on. He said

"The new wave is, like my ghost

back in black waves." The wrong sense

of play. A torch surged and blessed

a small phrase of flame. The mind's knife

knew no want; it still kissed me

dead eye, the mind's still skin of sight

tone deaf tongue. First snow

drift of fleas in the last light

large truck on the hill

I am thin king of the new self

blue lines that cross arms. We pass on

gnats in bits and rags, small cult

be like God. Be on call

myth leads to more myth

a mess, built like blood, by and by

A bell in the night sky. Up

the day shook. You were on the grass

screwed. You were born here

in this aisle. So cold, soul. Sell the pups

sleep in late. June is on. Jack slept

on a rose and woke up. Now

he had signs, juice for his day trip

she loved me for an hour this time

we went to the blue house

to see the brown man cry

what was there was found but not

brought to light. A sex hat

two lone deer. A wall of snow

drugs. At first I missed the view

then her dress, and then (at last) my sense

I could still hear my voice

low and still. As though a field

dead to my lips. The night

cut in half with a choir

and touch is a drug

and those who know how to touch well

will be taught (to be lit)

she stabbed my hand and I woke up

I bit her face and she broke down

the glass we wore we were

So much air. Grieved. A ball

on the roof. Shared doubts

a man made out of thought is

back on the chain, gang. He is our years

stirred air, blue. Beer in the fridge

bugs in the fudge. A tray of meat

speaks. The vague shapes

drag out their knives. What sails out

a doubt to fix these things

Grace comes to the beat

where we stand. Grace takes

out the sneer. In such a mind

one learns what leans

my lad, my hard man in spring

your weeks look cool in the clear

fair words, more flux, a flock

dragged out of wood. A gun that fits

a purse, a real space spun from what

it's real small. It realms all its wants

it has a grip and so on

my push is sent to the best of you

notes on verse in prose and the rest

drop down your wings. Show them off

your sure feet. Our roots shared

in time, not place. Gods are men first

then they are dogs or sounds

the joke is that it kills. The real gig

what that is. I can feel the floor, a flow

I blame the girl. She chews on a mask

as though glass is age is ash

the night looks down and says touch

a long threat. A night moves

for lengths of time I am my hands

To whom I have crawled

in whose sheets I flit

A dish of green things. A sense

of calm in a pose. A new sleep

a hand on her thigh, in the stream

the ink froze. Put it in the boat

no one moves, no one pays at the pump

my eyes. Sex rules. Weird cheer

more form. A new judge

it's the play of the mind

in a cage by the shades. It is wed

by the wind to the reed

like veins in a bird of prey

a black robe. The oath was weighed

the toy words were scales

the fries were gold. Aches

and flecks. Moon shakes. Flag

shit. Bent like so much depth

drunk on the drift

clean lines next to God lines

a stag in a pond in a sharp spin

notes. Not of the soul. The soil

as a sun. A death rat. The sun's fan

a sign fall. Look to the sun

clean lines. A fear of the known

NOTES

The title "Imaginary Synonyms" is taken from the poem "Eccentricity of the Middle Ground" by Mary Margaret Sloan.

"World Jelly" was intentionally patterned after the poems of Chris Vitiello, the lyrics of Robert Pollard and Bob Dylan, and the haiku of Jack Kerouac. The title "World Jelly" was created by the Guided by Voices Song Title Generator.

Some scaffolding for *"Complex Sleep"* was provided by the Beatles, Standard Schaefer, Louis Zukofsky, Can, Richard Buckner, Charles Olson, Sarah Manguso, Lou Reed, the Rolling Stones, Edgar Lee Masters, GBV, Frank Stanford, Jimmie Rodgers, Bob Dylan, Curtis Mayfield, Paul Simon, CCR, Captain Beefheart, Leonard Cohen, Brakhage, Eno, Paul Mann, Ella Jenkins, Ronald Johnson, H.D., Paul White, Wittgenstein, Gertrude Stein, Mt. Cleverest (Zachary Wait, Dea Self, Amy Wolfe), Chris Stamey, Dora Maar, Jack Spicer, Solomon Linde, Joseph Donahue, Todd Sandvik, Chris Vitiello, Jackson Mac Low, Sebadoh, Althea & Donna. The original *"Complex Sleep"* itself exists now only in memory, or in a perpetual state of potentiality. It no longer exists.